Vehicle
Coloring Book

Copyright © 2017 by DP Kids
All rights reserved. This book or any portion thereof
may not be reproduced or used in any manner whatsoever without the express
written permission of the publisher
except for the use of brief quotations in a book review.
First edition: 2017
Photo credit: Shutterstock

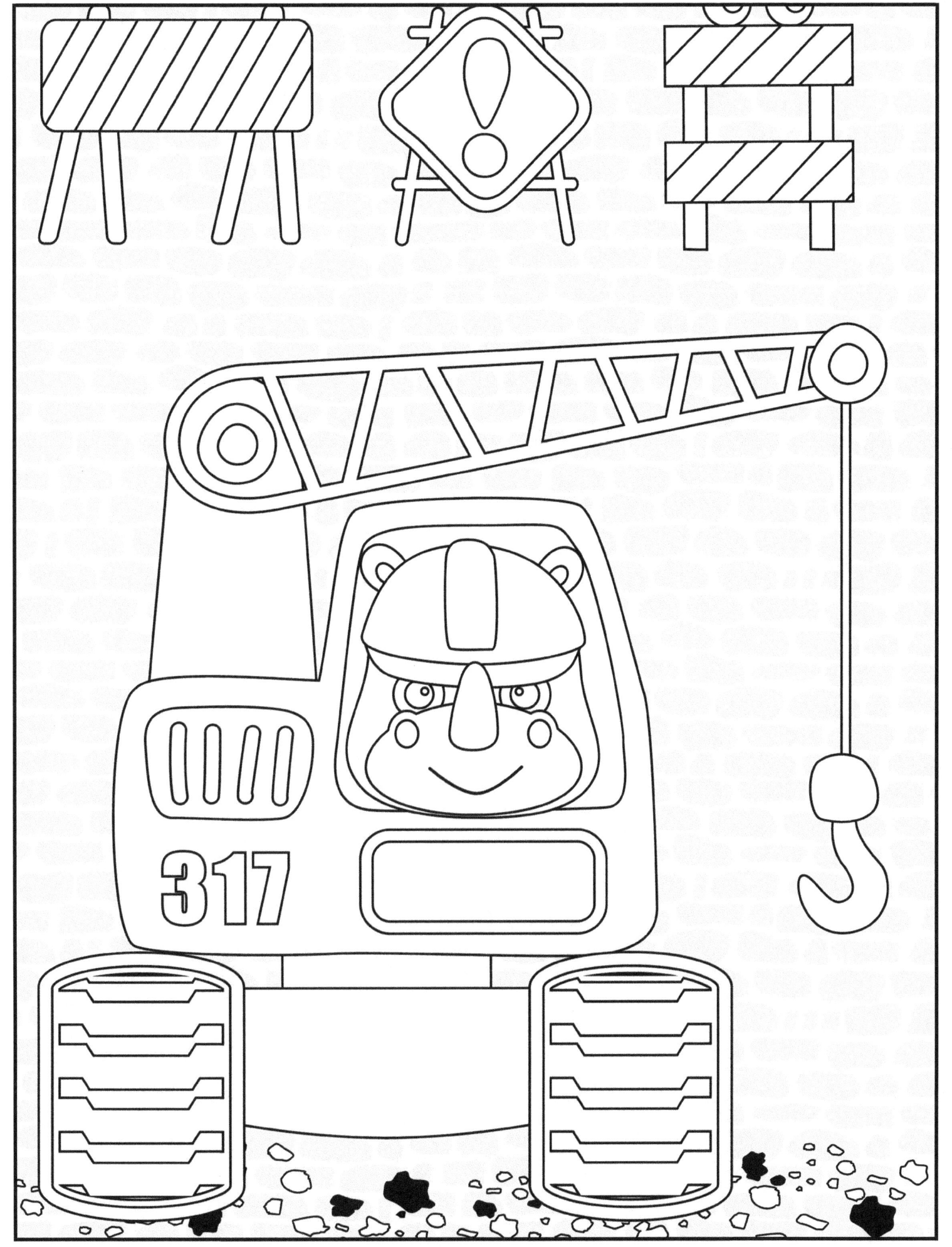

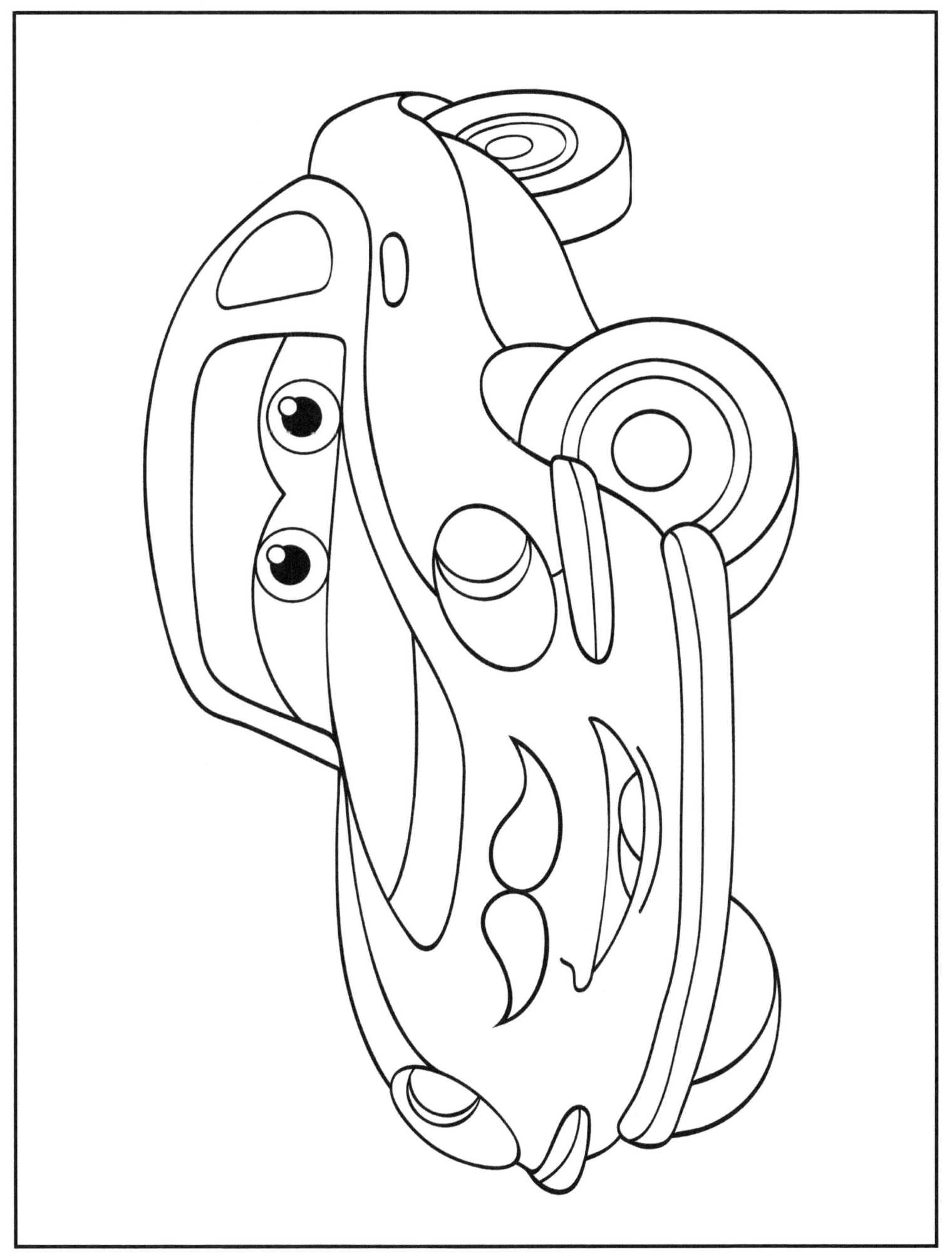

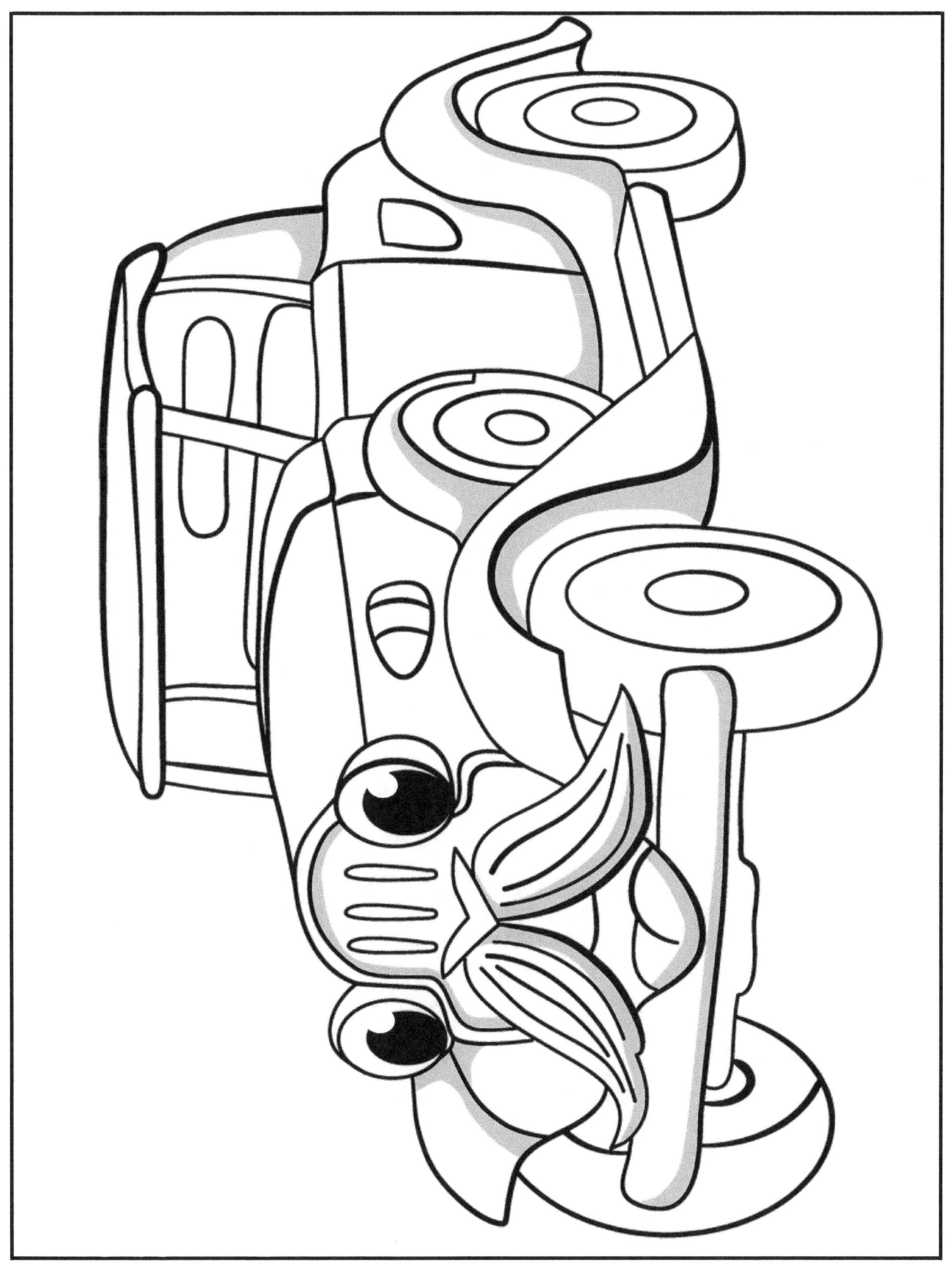

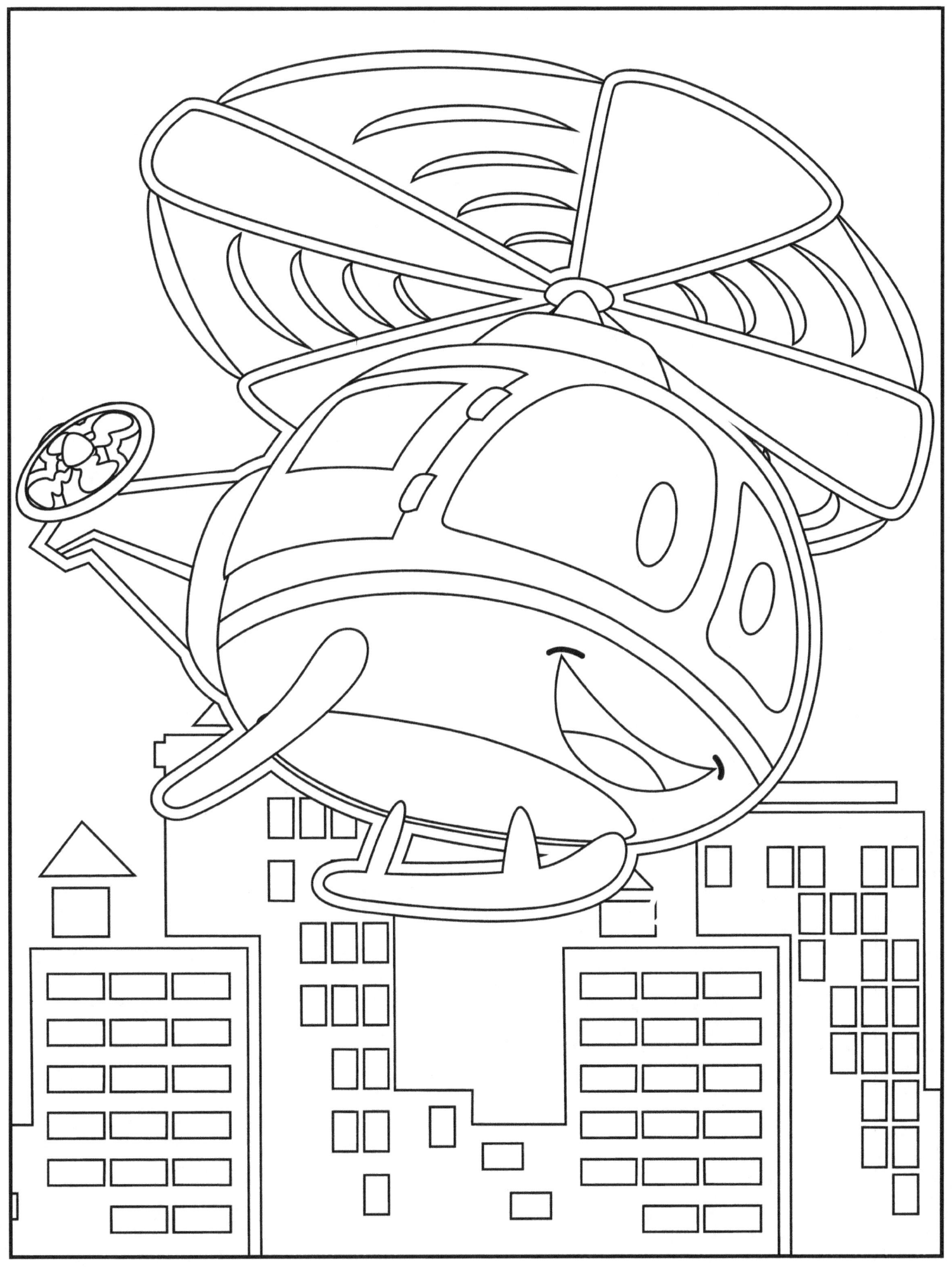

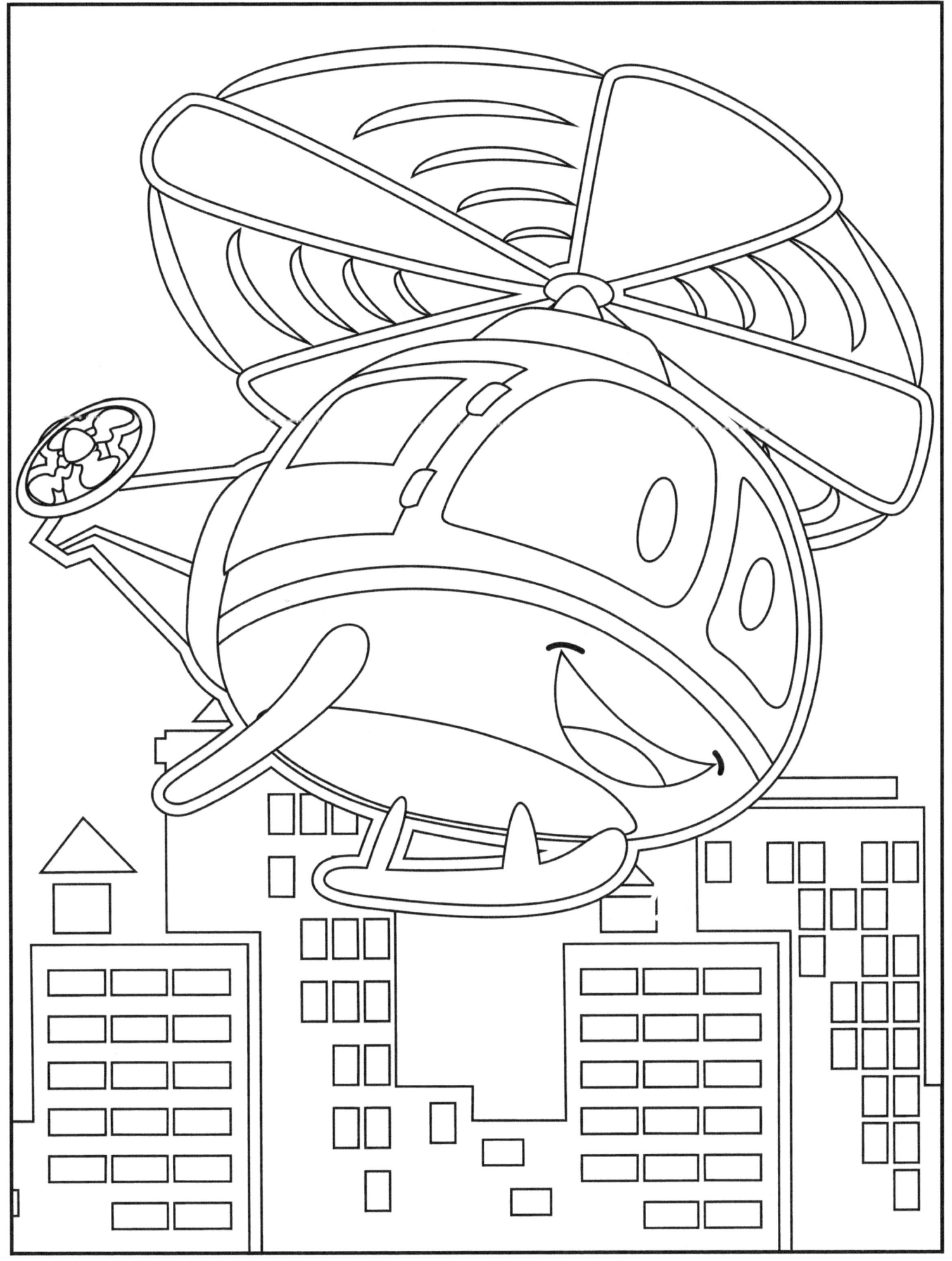

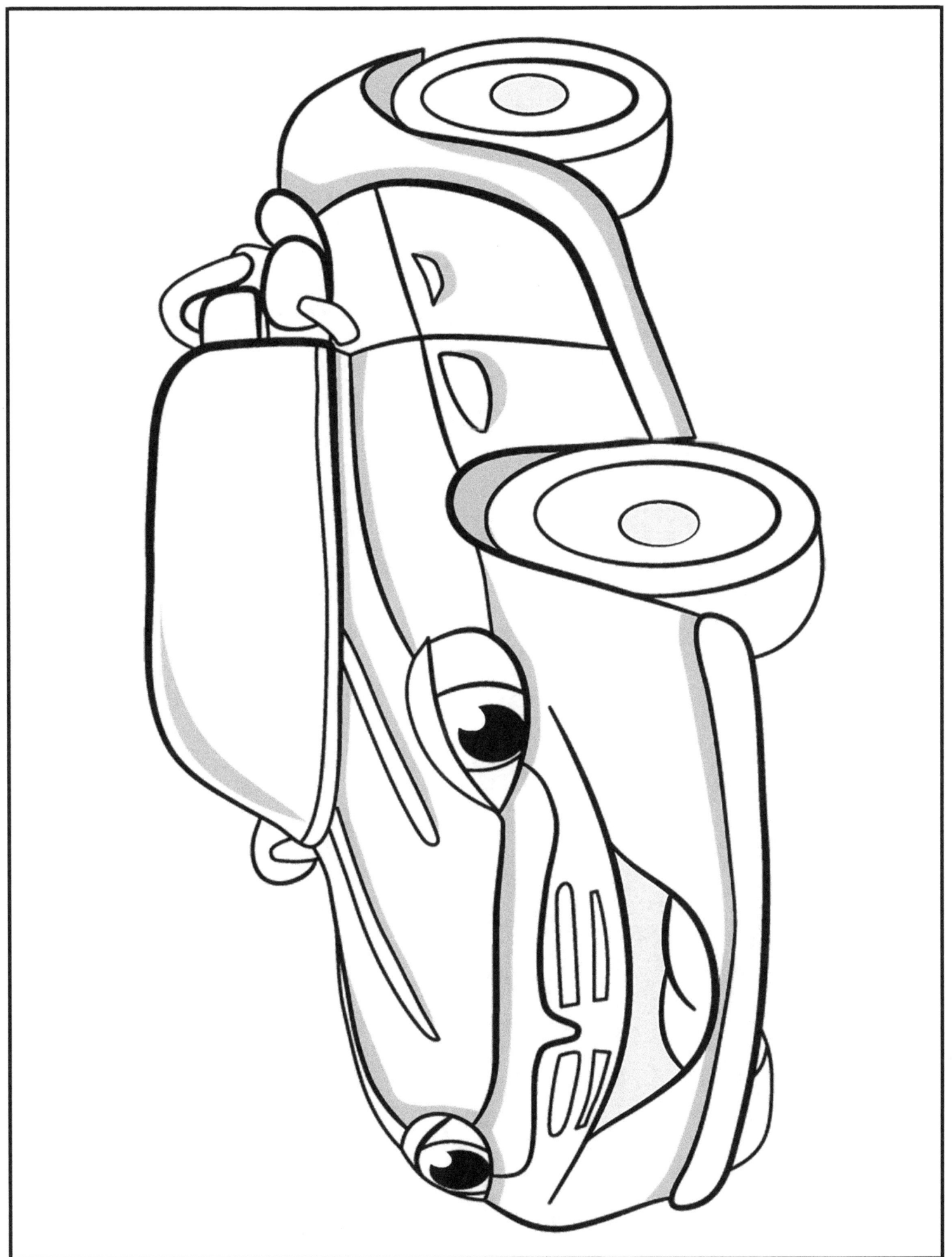

Bonus

Turn the page for bonus pages from some of our most popular coloring and activity books.

TRUCK
COLORING BOOK

COLORING BOOKS FOR KIDS

Connect the Dots
Book for Kids

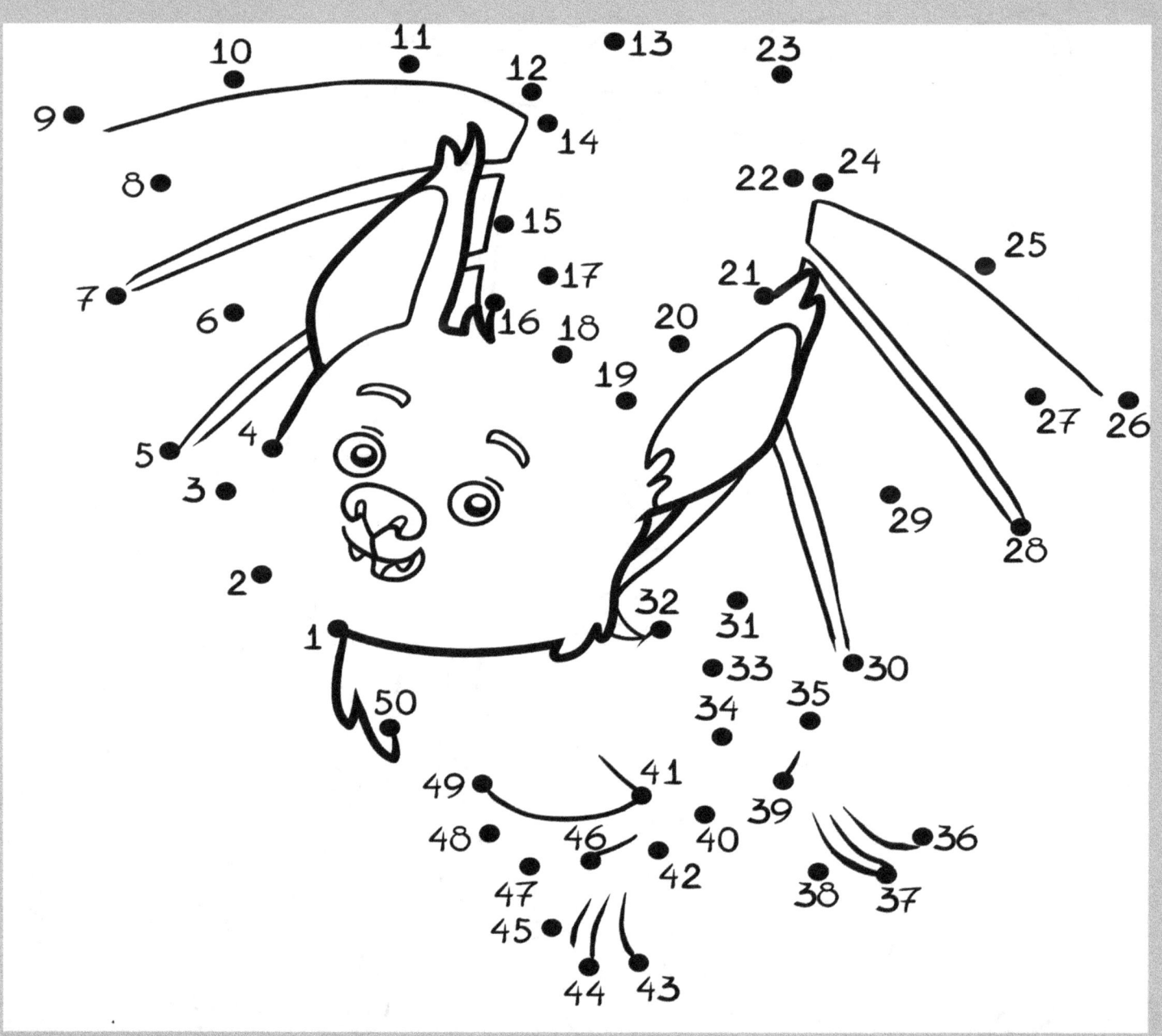

Challenging and Fun Dot to Dot Puzzles

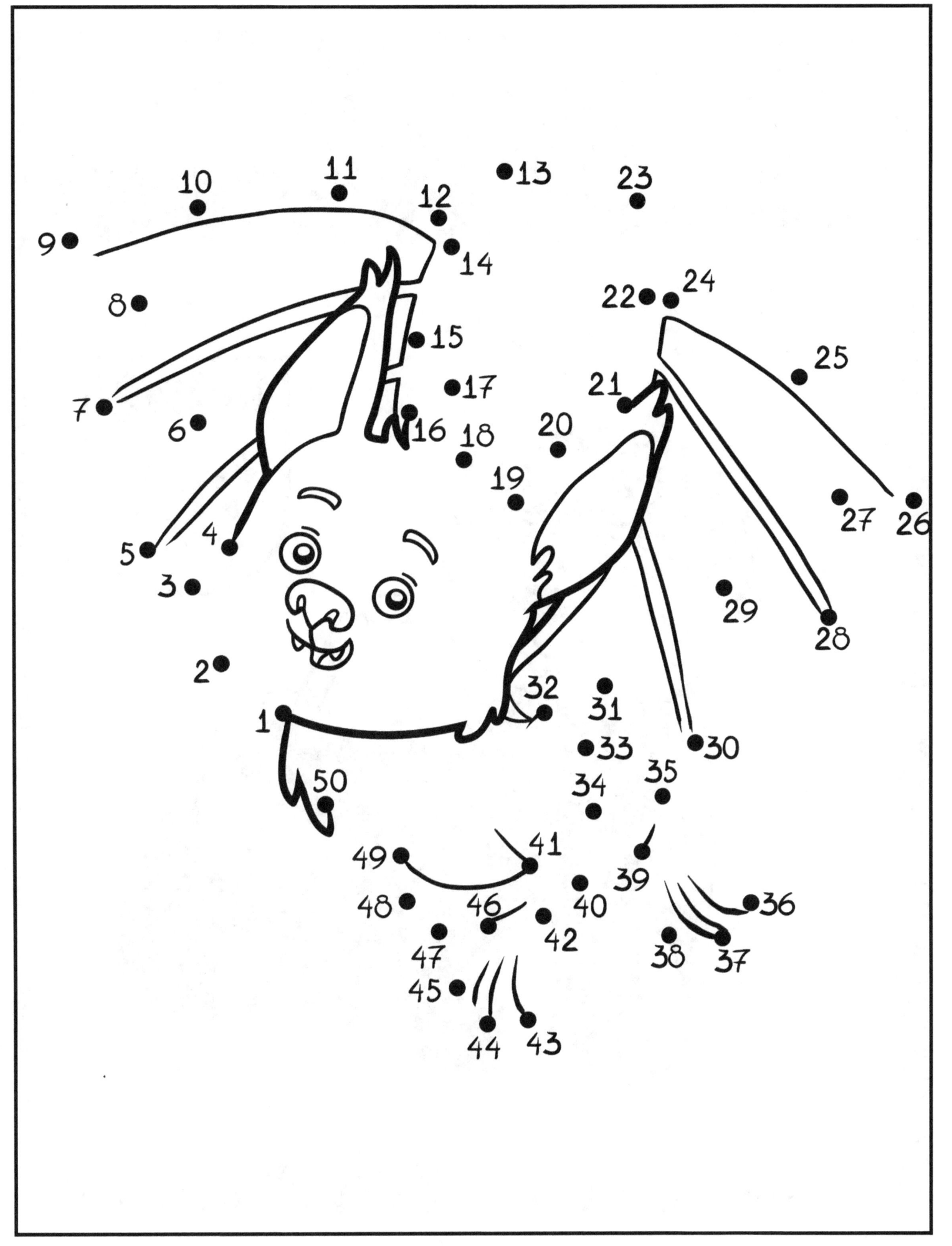

www.ingramcontent.com/pod-product-compliance
Lightning Source LLC
Chambersburg PA
CBHW081354080526
44588CB00016B/2490